VERONA
2024

Travel Guide

Kathleen J. Hale

Copyright © 2024 by Kathleen J. Hale

All rights reserved. No part of this publication may be reproduced, distributed, or transmitted in any form or by any means, including photocopying, recording, or other electronic or mechanical methods, without the prior written permission of the publisher, except in the case of brief quotations embodied in critical reviews and certain other noncommercial uses permitted by copyright law.

TABLE OF CONTENTS

MAP OF VERONA	5
WELCOME TO VERONA	6
VERONA HISTORY	8
WEATHER IN VERONA	10
CHAPTER 1	13
GETTING AROUND VERONA	13
PUBLIC TRANSPORT	13
THINGS TO SEE IN VERONA	15
PIAZZA BRA	15
BASILICA OF SAN ZENO MAGGIORE	17
CASTELVECCHIO MUSEUM	18
GIARDINO DI PALAZZO GIUSTI	19
TORRE DEI LAMBERTI AND THE GALLERIA D'ARTE MODERNA ACHILLE FORTI	20
ROMAN THEATRE AND ARCHAEOLOGICAL MUSEUM	22
CASA GIULIETTA	23
ARENA DI VERONA	24
MUSEUM OF NATURAL HISTORY	25
CHIESA DI SANT'ANASTASIA	26
TOURIST OFFICES	27
THINGS TO DO IN VERONA	**28**
ENJOY AN ATMOSPHERIC DISPLAY IN A ROMAN ARENA	28
HOP ABOARD A LAKE GARDA FERRY AND DISCOVER THE SURROUNDING CITIES.	29
TOUR THE TOWN CENTER ON WHEELS	30

BEST THINGS TO DO IN VERONA, ITALY — 31

Criuse the Funicular to Piazzale Castel San Pietro	32
Take a Walking Food Tour	33
Walk Through an Arch to Piazza dei Signori	35
Pay Respect to the Scaliger Tombs	36
Climb Lamberti Tower	37
Tour Juliet's House and Balcony	38
Visit the Roman Theater and Archaeological Museum	39
Explore Castelvecchio Castle and Museum	40
Look at the Opera at Fondazione Arena di Verona	41
Wander Through Giardino Giusti	42
Take a Day Trip to Lake Garda	43
Say a Prayer at Duomo di Verona	44
Stoll Around Piazza Bra	46
Verona excursions and tours	47
Walking tours	47
Shopping in Verona	49
Shopping centers	51
Restaurants in Verona	52
Verona Nightlife	57
Bars in Verona	58
Clubs in Verona	60
Live music in Verona	61
Italy Food and Drink	64

CHAPTER 2 — 67

Travel To Verona	**67**
Flying To Verona	67
Verona Hotels	70

CHAPTER 4 — 77

ITALY INFORMATION	**77**
ITALY VISA AND PASSPORT REQUIREMENTS	78
EXTENSION OF STAY	84
ENTRY WITH PETS	84
ITALY HEALTH CARE AND VACCINATIONS	86
FOOD AND DRINK	87
CURRENCY AND MONEY	87
CONCLUSION	91

MAP OF VERONA

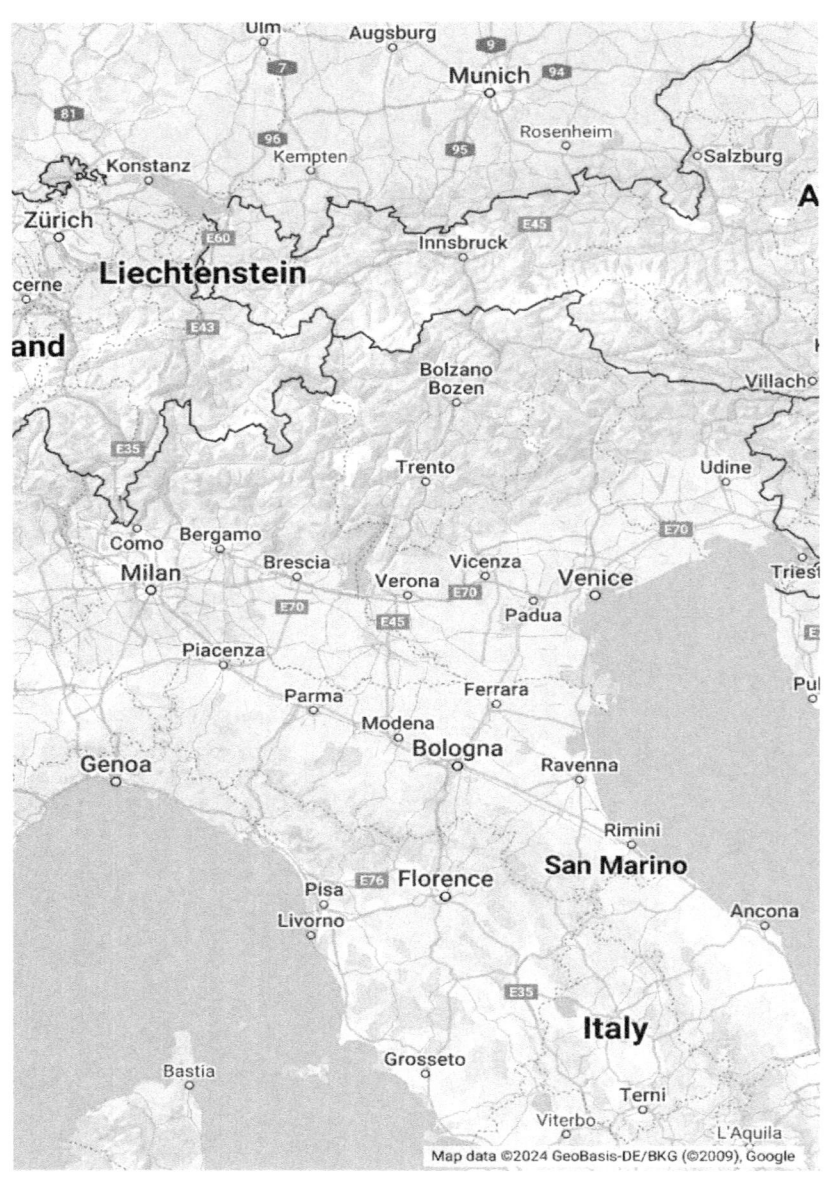

WELCOME TO VERONA

Verona, the setting for history's most famous love story, has so much more to explore than Romeo and Juliet. Romance, passion, conflict, and love shaped this city. However, its Roman, medieval, and Renaissance architectural treasures made it a UNESCO World Heritage designation.

Verona is known for its impressively preserved architecture. Its magnificent amphitheater - the Arena - has remained unchanged for over two centuries. Verona's summer opera festival still draws 25,000 spectators to the marble seats.

Verona, also known as Piccolo Roma or Little Rome, is a city of narrow streets and beautiful baroque buildings.

Its historical monuments and many restaurants make it the perfect place for a weekend getaway.

Roman gates and sections of the original wall are everywhere. The elegant three-story Porta is above Corso Porta Borsari. This shopping street has the best of everything.

Romeo and Juliet are the ones who have left the most lasting mark. Find out about the love and pain of lovers on the 14th-century balcony at Casa di Giulietta. They have left their hopeful messages on the courtyard wall.

Romeo's expulsion took place on the Cortile del Mercato Vecchio. In the epilogue, visitors will find Juliet's grave in the crypt in San Francisco al Corso.

Verona boasts several stunning churches. With its soft yellow stone and elegant arches, the Basilica of San Zeno Maggiore has been hailed as one of the world's finest Romanesque structures.

Castelvecchio, an ancient castle overlooking the Valpolicella and Soave wine regions, rises above the city. The Via Mazzoni is great for browsing boutique shops, designer chains, and buzzing market stalls.

Verona, located in the wealthy Veneto region (northeastern Italy), is just a few hours away by train or car from Venice, Vicenza, and Padua. This makes Verona a good base for exploring this beautiful and historic area of Italy.

VERONA HISTORY

According to records, Verona has been a place of settlement since about 550 BC. Since she became a Roman settlement in the first century BC, its location, which straddled the major east-west and south-north trade routes, made it a crucial base for the Roman Empire, which built impressive amphitheaters and grand gateways.

After the fall of Rome, Verona's strategic location attracted other regional powers. it was conquered by Ostrogoths, Lombards, and Charlemagne. In the 13th century, it was finally under the control of the Scaliger family.

The family may have been tyrants, but they fortified Verona and extended its influence on Vincenza and

Treviso. The family was also a great patron of the arts. In the 13th and 14th centuries, Dante, Petrarch, and Giotto flourished in this city, which experienced a golden age of prosperity and peace.

Verona fell under Venetian control in the 15th century after family feuds, fratricides, and other factors. Under their rule, the Porta Nuova, Porta Palio, and Piazza Bra were built and ruled by Venice until Napoleon's army swept across the peninsula in 1797. Verona became Austria's war trophy and only escaped foreign dominance during the unification of Italy.

A terrible flood in 1882 destroyed much of the historical center, necessitating the building of high walls to protect the city. However, they were not strong enough to withstand the bombs dropped by the Allies during WWII, which caused further damage to the town.

All the bridges and 40% of the city's buildings were demolished and destroyed as the Germans retreated. The extensive and long reconstruction made it possible to achieve restoration. Verona survived enough to be designated a UNESCO World Heritage Site in 2000.

Nevertheless, much of the original Verona Arena, built in AD30, remains intact—but an earthquake in 1117 destroyed the theater's outer part.

History has it that rubbing the right breast on a statue of Juliet at Juliet's House will bring luck to those unlucky with love. However, the bronze statue was replaced in 2014 after the caressing had damaged it.

Verona was a part of Austrian Venetia from 1866 until it joined the Kingdom of Italy.

Weather in Verona

Verona has a temperate and warm climate and receives a lot of rain. It is in northern Italy, and it's best to avoid winter. The weather is cold, and many of the activities around Lake Garda are closed.

The winter (December to January) is the driest season. Temperatures hover at an average of around 6 degrees Celsius.

The weather is great in spring and fall, but the city is quiet. The spring (March to May) is characterized by heavy rain, with the wettest months being May, and temperatures reaching up to 22 degrees Celsius.

Autumn (September-November) is characterized by heavy rain, but temperatures remain pleasant at an average of 18degC.

The opera season is in July and August when temperatures reach above 30 degrees Celsius. If you want to go during the summer, book well in advance.

CHAPTER 1

Getting Around Verona

Public Transport

Verona has a very good public transportation system. ATV (Tel. +39 045 805.7811 http://www.atv.verona.it/ operates a reliable and frequent bus service in the city. Daily bus passes are available.

Taxis

You can only pick up taxis at designated taxi stands throughout the city, including the railway station, Piazzabra, and the taxi ranks at the airport.

Pre-book a cab by calling Taxi & Autoblu at +39 045 858 1403 or Unione Radiotaxi at +39 045 532666. The meter will start to run after you book the taxi, not when you pick it up.

Some of the hotel staff will also be willing to arrange taxis. They usually arrive within minutes, and it is customary to leave a small tip.

Driving

Verona's historic center has several traffic restrictions that can make driving painful. Be aware of parking signs if you drive. Unlike in other Italian cities, you will get a ticket. Blue road markings denote pay-and-display parking. Tickets can be purchased at the nearest tobacconist or the nearest meter. Piazza Cittadella is the most convenient parking area.

Hire a car

You can hire a car at the airport, but the driver must be eligible to drive, have a validated credit card, and have a European driver's license or an International Driver's Permit. Avis, Europcar, and Hertz are all recommended car rental companies at the airport.

Local companies within the city include Morini Rent (Tel: +39 0289 550 840; www.morinirent.com/en) and the more upmarket Autonoleggio Oliosi Di Ferron Giancarlo & Andrea (Tel: +39 045 581 188; www.autonoleggioliosi.com).

Bicycle rental

Verona's bike share scheme is a great way to get around. Verona Bike, the city's bikeshare program (tel. 800 896 948 in Italy; +39 24546 7898 internationally; www.bikeverona.it), has stations at the Piazza Bra and the Castelvecchio Museum, among other locations.

Bicycle hire is also available from La Bici i, Via San Lucillo 18 (Tel: +39 45 890 4249; www.labiciverona.it).

Things To See In Verona

Piazza Bra

The central Piazza is dominated by the Arena's impressive walls and the elegant neoclassical frontage of the Palazzo Municipale. It has been at the heart of Veronese culture for centuries. Cafés and restaurants with pastel-colored buildings surround the Piazza, making it ideal for an aperitivo and watching Veronese culture.

Address: Piazza Bra, Verona, 37121 Telephone:

Opening hours:

Every day, 24 hours.

Admission Charges: No

Disabled access: Yes

UNESCO: No

Basilica of San Zeno Maggiore

The Romanesque style was developed in Italy between the 1120s to the 1930s. It is a large building with an impressive bell tower that Dante Alighieri mentioned in Divine Comedy. There are frescoed interior walls and a crypt containing the remains of Saint Zeno. The crypt is said to be the location of Shakespeare's Romeo & Juliet's marriage.

Address: Vicolo Abbazia 1, Piazza San Zeno, Verona, 37121

Telephone: +39 45 800 6120.

Opening hours: Mon-Sat, 0830-1800 and Sun, 1230-1800.

Website: http://www.basilicasanzeno.it

Admission Charges: Yes

Disabled access: Yes

UNESCO: No

Castelvecchio Museum

This castle, built in the 14th century by the della Scala, was a military fortress until 1925 when it was converted to a residence. Weapons and jewelry are still on display, but the medieval frescoes by Pisanello Veronese Tintoretto and other treasures make this castle so interesting.

Address: Corso Castelvecchio, 2, Verona, 37121

Telephone: +39 45 806 2611

Opening hours: Tue-Sun 0830-1930, Mon 1330-1930.

Website: http://museodicastelvecchio.comune.verona.it

Admission fee: Yes

Disabled access: Yes

UNESCO: Yes

Giardino di Palazzo Giusti

Giardino Giusti is one of the most beautiful Renaissance Gardens in Italy. Behind the palace of that name, it is a sprawling estate with flowers, statues, fountains, an avenue lined with cypress trees, and Europe's first labyrinth. It was built in the late 16th Century but has seen many renovations.

Address: Via Giardino Giusti 2, Verona, 37129

Telephone: +39 45 803 4029.

Opening hours: Daily 0900-1900

Website: http://www.grandigiardini.it

Admission Charges: Yes

Disabled access: Yes

UNESCO: No

Torre dei Lamberti and the Galleria d'Arte Moderna Achille Forti

Climb the 84m-high (276ft) medieval Torre dei Lamberti (Lamberti Tower) for spectacular views across Verona. You can take the lift most of the time but must use your breath for the last few stories. Tickets include entry to the Galleria d'Arte Moderna Achille Fori (Gallery of Modern Art), which houses a wonderful collection of regional contemporary artwork from the 19th to the 21st centuries.

Address: Cortile Mercato Vecchio, Verona, 37121

Contact: +39 45927 3303 (Lamberti Tower); +39 45800 1903 (Gallery of Modern Art).

Opening hours: Tue-Fri 0900-1715, Sat-Sun 1100-1815.

Website: http://gam.comune.verona.it/nqcontent.cfm?a_id=42701

Admission Charges: Yes

Disabled access: No

UNESCO: No

Roman Theatre and Archaeological Museum

The Roman Theatre is located north of Old Town and dates from the 1st Century BC. In the late 19th century, it was used to stage ballets and plays. After being abandoned for centuries, it was restored and reopened. Located in a former medieval Jesuit convent, the Archaeological Museum has been closed for renovation.

Address: Regaste Redentore 2, Verona, 37129

Telephone: +39 45 800 0360.

Opening hours: Mon 1330-1830, Tues-Sun 0830-1830.

Admission Charges: Yes

Disabled access: Yes

UNESCO: No

Casa Giulietta

Although the Capulets lived in Verona, it is unlikely that they ever lived at Casa Giulietta. The balcony was only built in the 1920s to please visitors. A statue of Juliet is in the courtyard.

Casa Romeo is the actual home of Romeo. It can be found on Arche Scaligere 4, but the Montague family occupied it. It is not accessible to the public.

Address: Cappello 23 (Casa Giuilietta), Verona, 37121

Telephone: +39 45 803 4303

Opening hours: Mon 1330-1930, Tue-Sun 0830-1930.

Admission Charges: Yes

Disabled access: Yes

UNESCO: No

Arena di Verona

The Arena in Verona has a capacity for 25,000 people, making it the largest Roman amphitheater in northern Italy. It was built early in the 1st Century AD and has seen gladiatorial battles, public executions, concerts, and operas. Every summer, it hosts the city's famous opera festival.

Address: Piazza Bra, Verona, 37121

Telephone: +39 45 800 3204.

Opening hours:

Open times are listed on the website.

Website: http://www.arena.it

Admission Charges: Yes

Disabled access: Yes

UNESCO -Yes

Museum of Natural History

Museo di Storia Naturale will keep natural history enthusiasts busy for hours. The 16 spacious rooms are filled with scientific and historical finds in sections such as botany and geology. The museum occupies the Palazzo Pompei, the former home of the wealthy family Lavezzola, and was built between 1530 and 1550.

Address: Central Verona, Lungadige Porta Vittoria 9, Verona, 37129

Telephone: +39 45 807 9400.

Opening hours: Mon-Thurs 0900-1700, Sat-Sun 1400-1800.

Website: http://www.museostorianaturaleverona.it

Admission Charges: Yes

Disabled access: Yes

UNESCO: No

Chiesa di Sant'Anastasia

Verona's biggest church was built between 1290 and 1481 and is home to some of the city's finest art. The bare exterior hides a rich interior of frescoes. Pisanello created a fresco that tells the story of S George Freeing the Princess from the Dragon.

Address: Piazza di Sant'Anastasia, Verona, 37121

Telephone: +39 45 592 813.

Opening hours: Mon-Fri 0900-1830, Sat 0900-1800, Sun 1300-1800 (Mar-Oct); Mon-Fri 1000-1700, Sun 1300-1700 (Nov-Feb).

Website: http://www.chieseverona.it

Admission Charges: Yes

Disabled access: Yes

UNESCO: No

Tourist Offices

IAT Verona

Address: Piazza Bra, via degli Alpini 9, Verona, 37121

Telephone: +39 45 806 8680.

Opening hours: Mon-Sat 0900-1800, Sun 1000-1600.

Website: http://www.tourism.verona.it

IAT Verona has a friendly and small tourist office. It sells English-language guides and offers several free maps, including a shopping guide and one that provides information about the most important historical sites. Another tourist office is in the Verona Porta Nuova station, Piazza XXV.

Tourist Passes

VeronaCard http://www.veronacard.it/. With this card, you can get free or discounted entrance to the museums, churches, and attractions in Verona. Visitors can purchase a pass for one or three days. The card is available at museums and tourist information offices.

Things To Do In Verona

Enjoy An Atmospheric Display In A Roman Arena

One of the most outstanding venues in Italy is Arena Di Verona (Tel: +39 458 05 151; http://www.arena.it/), a first-century Roman amphitheater whose doors show some of the finest worldwide. It seats 30,000 people and has a summer festival that includes opera, ballet, and concert performances. Winter visitors should check out Verona's outstanding Teatro Filarmonico.

Hike its coastline, then cool your feet in Lake Garda.

Along with an adorable city center, Verona is surrounded by a useful resource and a wealth of walking possibilities. For extremely good hikes, walk along the beaches of Lake Garda, at the same time as the trek from Il Vittoriale botanical gardens in Gardone Riviera to the Valtenesi vineyards is rewarded with a chilly glass of neighborhood Chiaretto (rosé wine).

Hop aboard a Lake Garda ferry and discover the surrounding cities.

Nearby Lake Garda encompasses a massive 370 square km (142 square miles). The Brenta Dolomites enhance to the north, while its southern slight hills feature a Mediterranean microclimate. The big lake is high-quality and explored by boat, so hop on a Navigazione sul Lago di Garda's (Tel: +800 551 801, in Italy most effective; http://www.navigazionelaghi.it/ ferry and discover its surrounding towns.

Speed at some stage in Lake Garda using wind strength.

It might take a little while to discover that windsurfing is one of the most famous sports on Lake Garda. Blessed with crystal-clean water and extraordinarily dependable wind conditions, surfers set out from Torbole, Riva del Garda, and Garda metropolis. Surf Center Marco Segnana (Tel: +39 464 505 963; http://www.surfsegnana.it/) has everything windsurfers require, including amateur instruction.

Tour The Town Center On Wheels

With abundant greenery and well-marked paths, the river Adige makes a tremendous wheel break out from the metropolis. Now, it is not that major Verona is without its biking charms. Verona Bike is a bicycle percentage scheme, and it's remarkable for gliding among ancient points of interest, specifically considering the center's traffic policies.

Best Things to Do in Verona, Italy

Remember that one of Italy's most popular journey locations for love is Verona, between Milan and Venice in northern Italy's Veneto place. Verona is famously called the putting for William Shakespeare's "Romeo and Juliet." Still, it is also home to numerous historic and modern-day points of interest.

From touring the precise home of the Roman Forum at Piazza delle Erbe to looking at the opera in a genuine Roman area, you'll discover masses of inspiring sports on your trip to Verona anytime in twelve months.

Criuse the Funicular to Piazzale Castel San Pietro

Address: Piazzale Castel San. Pietro, 37129 Verona VR, Italy

The Castel San Pietro sits at the pinnacle of the hill. He is on the market by foot or with a current-day automated funicular. From the top of the mountain, you could capture one of the most picturesque views of the metropolis. If you do choose to walk, it's an incredible opportunity to apprehend all the small homes and quiet streets from the manner up.

Visitors can revel in the views from the square; however, the castle isn't open to the public. Still, it has an interesting history worth learning about, from its origins because of the online website of a Roman fortress to the existing construction's nineteenth-century manufacturing.

Take a Walking Food Tour

Typical dishes of Verona include the whole thing from minced pork with Risotto and pasta with beans, and you may spend weeks right here attempting all the wonderful specialties. A strolling meal and wine tour is in order if you run on a mile-short timeline.

Ways Tours offers a pinnacle-rated excursion led by a guide who will show you the metropolis' essential landmarks while guiding you through espresso, pastries, and Valpolicella wine tastings.

Going with a guide guarantees you get an inside-of-the-scenes look at actual Italian kitchens to see how pasta is made and a neighborhood professional reachable at the wine preserve that will help you determine the great vintages to take domestic.

Go to the Roman Forum at Piazza delle Erbe.

ADDRESS: Piazza Erbe, 46100 Mantova MN, Italy

To begin your enjoyment with a chunk of records, head to the authentic net web page of the Roman Forum, Piazza delle Erbe. This square Piazza is located inside the coronary heart of historical Verona and is surrounded by lovely medieval buildings and towers. You will discover a 14th-century fountain crowned with a Roman-fashion statue in its middle.

Although it was soon used as a key area to promote produce and homemade gadgets, most stalls at Piazza delle Erbe now offer traveler souvenirs instead. However, you'll also locate small cafes where you could have coffee in the morning or a pitcher of wine to give up the day along one aspect of the Piazza.

Walk Through an Arch to Piazza dei Signori

ADDRESS: Piazza dei Signori, 37121 Verona VR, Italy

WEB: http://www.Turismoverona.Ecu/nqcontent.Cfm?A_id=35987

From Piazza delle Erbe, walk past Arco della Costa, an arch with a whale rib, and put it into Piazza dei Signori, a small square surrounded by considerable houses. In the middle is a statue of Dante, and perched atop homes across the square are extra famous signori.

This rectangular became the seat of the metropolis's public establishments. You may come across the tower of the Palazzo del Capitanio, the fifteenth-century Loggia del Consiglio that was the metropolis corridor, and the 14th-century Palazzo della Prefettura, previously the Palazzo del Governo that became a residence of the Scaligeri own family.

Pay Respect to the Scaliger Tombs

ADDRESS: Via Santa. Maria Antica, 4, 37121 Verona VR, Italy

PHONE +39 05 806 2611

Web: https://museodicastelvecchio.Comune.Verona.It/nqcontent.Cfm?A_id=47849

One of the most influential households in the history of Verona, the Scaligers dominated the metropolis at some point in the 13th and 14th centuries. As a result, several monuments have been built around Verona, which include the Scaliger Tombs. This employer of five

Gothic funerary monuments is placed in a courtyard out of the doors of the church of Santa Maria Antica.

Every tomb is dedicated to a unique Verona's Lords: Cansignorio, Cangrande I, Mastino II, Alberto II, and Giovanni. The Scaliger Tombs are loose to enjoy and open every day of the year. Still, each tomb is separated from the road through a wall with iron bars that prevent vacationers from disturbing the lifeless lords that relax there.

Climb Lamberti Tower

ADDRESS: Verona VR, 1, 37121, Via della Costa, Italy

PHONE +39 05 927 3027

Web: http://www.Torredeilamberti.lt/

Located simply off Piazza delle Erbe close to Lamberti Tower-Torre d item Lamberti Palazzo della Ragione, it is an exceptional place to get a pinnacle stage view of Verona. Go up the stairs to the top or pay to take the elevator most of the way, and you could have notable views of the metropolis and past.

Construction for its medieval bell tower commenced in the 12th century; it was modified and raised sometimes until it reached its very last top of approximately 275 toes in 1436. Additionally, Count Giovanni Sagramoso introduced a clock to the tower in 1798 to replace the existing one close to Torre Gardello that had stopped working.

Tour Juliet's House and Balcony

ADDRESS: Via Cappello, 37121 Verona VR, Italy

The most well-known vacationer vacation spot in Verona, the 13th-century building called Juliet's House is a museum home dedicated to the titular female protagonist of Shakespeare's "Romeo and Juliet."

The house is a first-rate example of Gothic shape in the metropolis. In the museum, you will find a series of length furnishings to replicate what Juliet may want to have had in her home.

In a courtyard, off Via Capello-Juliet's House, is the famous balcony, where Romeo professed his likeness for the younger Juliet and a statue of Juliet herself. Visitors can view the balcony and bronze statue;

however, getting proper entry to the museum requires a low rate.

Alternatively, you could also see the residence attributed to Romeo's family on Via Arche Scaligere. Afterward, the traditional Verona meals, which include horse or donkey meat, are patterned at Osteria al Duca around the corner.

Visit the Roman Theater and Archaeological Museum

ADDRESS: Verona VR, Italy 2, 37129 Rigaste Redentore

PHONE +39 05 800 0360

Web: http://museoarcheologico.Comune.Verona.lt/

They are built right into a hill in front of the Adige River of the Roman Theater and Archaeological Museum for easy accessibility from Juliet's House through Ponte Pietra. This picturesque stone bridge crosses the river.

The 1st-century Roman theater here hosts outside performances in the summer, and the museum—housed within the former Convent of Saint Jerome—capabilities Roman mosaics, Etruscan and Roman bronze sculptures, and Roman inscriptions.

Both points of interest are open seven days each week, and tickets are required to get into everyone.

Explore Castelvecchio Castle and Museum

ADDRESS: Verona VR, Italy 2, 37121 Corso Castelvecchio

PHONE +39 05 806 2611

Web: https://museodicastelvecchio.Comune.Verona.It/

Built as a residence and forth in the 14th century, Castelvecchio is now a museum committed to medieval life in Verona. The building has numerous towers and is maintained with a brick bridge crossing the river.

The former parade floor interior is now a nice courtyard for the museum, which functions 16 rooms of the former palace packed with sacred art, paintings,

Renaissance bronze statues, archeological unearths, cash, weapons, and armor. Tours are available every day at some point in the year, and tickets are required to discover the museum.

Look at the Opera at Fondazione Arena di Verona

ADDRESS: P. Za Brà, Verona VR, Italy 1, 37121

PHONE +39 05 800 5151

Web: https://www.Area.lt/location/it

The town's biggest and most imposing monument, the Fondazione Arena di Verona, is the 0.33-largest Roman Arena in Italy after the region in Capua and the Colosseum in Rome.

Built-in the 1st century, it holds up to 250,000 spectators and now hosts many musical events, including Verona's leading opera companies and the celebrated opera competition known as the festival lirico all'Arena di Verona account of 1913.

However, the fine time to go to this Roman Arena is at some stage in the daylight while the solar shines brightly at the diploma.

Although some of the seating is now protected in brilliant orange and crimson chairs, it's easy to expect the precise appearance of the theater when it becomes used for less savory sports activities than watching a play or opera.

Wander Through Giardino Giusti

ADDRESS: Via Giardino Giusti, Verona VR, Italy 2, 37129

PHONE +39 05 803 4029

Web: http://giardinogiusti.Com/

It is located on the grounds of a big castle complicated at the Japanese seaside of the Adige River, Giardino Giusti, with a large spreading garden designed in the Italian Renaissance style and known as one of the high-quality examples of Italian gardens inside the U.S. Of the USA.

Along with 8 separate sections of gardens, this well-known attraction additionally functions as a hedge maze and a strolling trail through a small, wooded region on the point of the grounds. Throughout the 12 months, the Giusti Garden also opens to many activities, such as the Festival of Beauty, the Singing Garden, and rotating modern-day artwork exhibitions.

Take a Day Trip to Lake Garda

ADDRESS: Lake Garda, Italy

If you've got a chunk of time to discover spherical Verona, consider taking an afternoon walk to enjoy Lake Garda- Known as Lago di Garda in Italian. Lake Garda is one of Italy's most essential lakes. It is a well-known vacation spot for travelers and locals due to its crystal blue waters, extremely mild weather, and easy beaches.

The metropolis of Sirmione, placed at the south cease of the lake, is domestic to the towering fort referred to as Rocca Scaligera, which became as soon as owned by the influential Scaliger circle of relatives, as well as Grotte di Catullo, the stays of a Roman villa that used to exist at the peninsula. On the western shore in the city of Gardone Riviera, you may also discover the preceding home of poet d'Annunzio, Vittoriale degli Italiani.

Say a Prayer at Duomo di Verona

ADDRESS: Piazza Vescovado, 37121 Verona VR, Italy

PHONE +39 05 592813

WEB: http://www.Chieseverona.It/it/le-chiese/il-complesso-della-cattedrale

The Romanesque Cathedral, which is also known as Duomo di Verona, is a complex of homes that includes a twelfth-century Baptistery, the Canons Cloister, Saint Elena Church, and the stays of a 4th-century paleo-Christian Basilica.

The octagonal Romanesque baptismal font, embellished with carved Biblical scenes, was carved out of an unmarried solid piece of marble, and the Baptistery has frescoes from the 13th to fifteenth centuries. But the Cathedral's frescoes are from the 15th to 18th centuries, and the out of doors are embellished with 12th-century reliefs.

The Cathedral Complex is open on Sundays to Fridays for 12 months, with numerous hours via using season, and tickets are required to excursion the facilities. However, you could additionally see the internal of the cathedral at some point of spiritual offerings on Sundays free of charge, all three hundred and sixty-five days long.

Stoll Around Piazza Bra

ADDRESS: P. Za Brà, Verona VR, Italy

Once a suburban braid (discipline), Piazza Bra is a big piazza positioned inside the predominant gate getting into Verona. You'll see the Roman Arena on one aspect of the Piazza, close to the neoclassical Palazzo community, and several porticoed homes with cafes and eating places along a massive walkway on the alternative aspect. Piazza Bra is likewise home to an intensive garden with a major fountain, which makes for a wonderful place to take a picnic lunch or supply your carryout from one of the restaurants nearby.

Verona excursions and tours

Verona excursions

Walking tours

Juliet & Co. organize guided strolling tours of the historic metropolis center in English. There are some routes to be had, including Classic Verona, which covers the medieval part of the city, Romeo's House, the Scala circle of relative's residence and graves, plus Erbe Rectangular and its active market. Other tours encompass Shakespeare in Verona, Verona within the Moonlight, and Verona Noir, which recounts the city's dreadful past.

Tel: +39 347 034 3755

Website: http://www.Julietandco.Com

Bicycle tours

Veronality offers 3-hour guided bike tours of Verona in English. The excursion stops at all the top attractions, together with Castelvecchio, Verona Arena, Ponte Pietra, and Juliet's balcony. You'll additionally have the hazard to visit the principal squares and monuments even as listening to captivating and informative stories from your knowledgeable manual.

Tel: +39 0.5 221 8575

Website: http://www.Veronality.Com

Verona excursions

Valpolicella

Explore the Valpolicella district, a gentle, hilly panorama with numerous small valleys north of Verona that is famous for its satisfactory wines - the Valpolicella, the Amarone, and the Recioto. The landscape is sprinkled with captivating Romanesque churches, superb Palladian villas, wine cellars, fortresses, and parks. The region is justly famous for its cuisine, wherein boiled meat is an essential component.

Website: http://www.Valpolicella.It

Lake Garda

Lake Garda, situated 30km (18 miles) west of Verona, is a jewel among Italy's many lakes. Charming villages and small cities dot the landscape around the lake. To the south, the lake is characterized by way of gentle, Mediterranean-like slopes rising to the more dramatic steep hills and mountainsides in addition north. The lake is a hub for out of doors activities from mild walks and boat journeys to fishing, windsurfing, and diving. Ferries traverse the lake often. At Malcesine, the rotating cable automobile to Tratto Spine takes site visitors to a height of 760m (five 774ft) for outstanding perspectives.

Tel: +39 365 20636.

Website: http://www.Visitgarda.Com

Shopping in Verona

As a style-conscious, affluent city surrounded by skilled artisans and factories, Verona is a top-notch place for purchasing, the window variety. The historic center is peppered with exciting little boutiques. At the same time, the vicinity around Lake Garda is widely recognized for its discount fashion designer stores.

Luxury manufacturers, along with Gucci, Max Mara, Burberry, Givenchy, and Valentino, all have shops in the town. Still, the metropolis boasts male or woman producers and newly created labels.

Thanks to ages of skill with leatherwear, which makes Verona famed for its high nice shoe shops. There are also fragrance shops with exclusive mixes and numerous upcoming designers selling their wares.

A Foodie person will find a delectable variety of fresh pasta, herbs, dried oils, and salami in small, expert delis. Local wines and liqueurs are regularly available, too, complementing devilish Monte Veronese cheeses and heated breads.

Antique shops are in abundance nicely. However, good deal hunters must go to Piazza San Zeno on the 1/3 Saturday of the month for a vibrant and bustling flea market promoting jewelry, stamps, garments, and the occasional antique automobile.

Key regions

Via Mazzini is the most populous shopping avenue in Verona. Many of Italy's high avenue chains and massive logo names have stores right here. Via Mazzini may be located at the north end of Piazza Bra, and parallel to it runs the Corso Porta Borsari, which is also covered with fashion stores in addition to some exquisite shoe shops.

Markets

On Piazza delle Erbe, there may be a day-by-day marketplace with stalls promoting clothes, fruit, and greens (Mon-Sat 0800-1800). On Saturday morning, you'll also discover a huge flea market at the soccer stadium (0800-1400).

Shopping centers

Le Corte Venete, Viale del Commercio 1, is Verona's largest buying center. For an outsized trade complex, La Grande Mela, in Lugagnano, simply out of doors Verona, offers three floors and over a hundred thirty stores.

Opening hours

In popular, stores are open 0900-1930, with many smaller stores ultimate among 1300 and 1600. The whole lot is closed throughout August, on Thursday afternoon and Sunday. Many shops are frequently closed on Monday morning too.

Souvenirs

Head to Piazza delle Erbe to fill your suitcase with food, dried herbs, and wine, in addition to ornaments and vintage postcards. You'll also locate here and around about jewelry and add-ons if you're on the appearance out for trinkets and objects artwork to remind you of your life. Piazza Bra is another good preference in addition to Piazze delle Erbe. Most of the church buildings, which include the Basilica of San Zeno Maggiore, provide thrilling little pieces and keepsakes.

Tax statistics

Value-added tax (IVA) of 21% is introduced to each buy in Italy. If you're a non-EU resident and spend more than € hundred fifty-five on an unmarried object, then you could declare a reimbursement when you leave the

United States of America. The refund is handiest to be had from shops that show a 'tax unfastened Italy' (or similar) sign.

Restaurants in Verona

Verona has a humming eating place scene with an excellent blend of conventional Italian cooking and a few exciting, present-day takes on conventional delicacies. The food here is frequently meaty, even though fish is also widely available, and traffic can tuck into an enormous range of antipasti.

The Verona restaurants beneath have been grouped into 3 pricing categories:

Expensive (over €60)

Moderate (€30 to €60)

Cheap (up to €30)

These Verona eating place charges are for a three-direction meal for one with 1/2 a bottle of house wine or equivalent, tax, and carrier. Tipping is discretionary, but the suitable, ready body of workers needs to be rewarded with a few greater euros on top of the invoice.

Expensive

Il Desco

Cuisine: Italian

For a number of the best eating in Verona, if not in all of Italy, e-book a desk at Il Desco. Sit down in the refined art-lined dining room at one of the meticulously laid tables and sample chef Elia Rizzo's elegant regional northern delicacies. Highlights encompass brodo (pasta soup) with oysters and licorice ice cream.

Address: San Sebastiano 5/7, Verona, 37121

Telephone: +39 forty-five 595 358.

Website: http://www.Ildesco.Com

La Fontana

Cuisine: Contemporary Italian

This Michelin-starred eating place is located around the corner from the Arena. Two hundred years vintage, its interior is cluttered with pix and antiques, and its menu gives lots of conventional, nearby cooking with an emphasis on meat. Some lighter, more interesting versions are also covered with a remarkable tasting menu occasionally available too. The wine cellar is thrilling, with a wide selection of nearby labels and preference bottles from further afield.

Address: Portichetti Fontanelle three, Verona, 37121

Telephone: +39 45913 305.

Website: http://www.Ristorantelafontanina.Com

Ristorante Re Teodorico

Cuisine: Italian and European

It's tough to overcome this eating place's area and status because it is on a hill overlooking the Adige River and offers notable views of the city and its ancient Roman Theatre. A fashionable eating place with a stylish interior, Re Teodorico offers outstanding connoisseur cuisine drawing on conventional Continental and Italian cooking traditions. It is a unique region with a kitchen to match.

Address: Central Verona, Piazzale Castel San Pietro, 1, Verona, 37121

Telephone: +39 45 834 9903.

Website: https://reteodorico.Com/

Moderate

Al Pompiere

Cuisine: Italian

The fireman's hat - and then the restaurant is named - is still on the wall. Still, the cognizance of attention at this neighborhood institution is the good-sized array of neighborhood cheeses and the big hams dangling from the ceiling. You can, without difficulty, make a meal of the starters and charcuterie plate or attempt some of the precise nearby dishes consisting of oven-cooked beef with polenta or horsemeat stew.

Address: Vicolo Regina d'Ungheria 5, Verona, 37121

Telephone: +39 45 803 0537.

Website: http://www.Alpompiere.Com

Ristorante Apostoli

Cuisine: Italian

The twelve apostoli (apostles) were 12 businesspeople who might meet on this website within the late eighteenth century to discuss enterprise over wine and beneficient quantities of pasta. Something comparable has persisted till these days at this atmospheric and very traditional eating place, which has been run via the Gioco circle of relatives because early 1900s. Food served amid the frescos is hearty, and there's an emphasis on domestically made pasta and soups.

Address: Corticella San Marco, three, Verona, 37121

Telephone: +39 forty-five 596 999.

Website: http://www.12apostoli.Com

Ristorante Arche

Cuisine: Italian

One of Verona's most famous eating places, Ristorante Arche, is an incredible 130-year-old fish and seafood restaurant. The cuisine is modern-day but rooted in vintage Venetian cooking traditions. As Russian Nobel Prize winner for literature Joseph Brodsky as soon as said, the meals here exhibit 'historical flavors.' There is certainly something pure, authentic, or even archetypal about Ristorante Arche. For fish fanatics, it's miles possible to provide unforgettable enjoyment.

Address: Via Arche Scaligere 6, Verona, 37121

Telephone: +39 45 800 7415.

Website: http://www.Ristorantearche.Com

Cheap

Corte Farina

Cuisine: Italian

Super convenient after a hard afternoon buying on Via Mazzini, join the group of hungry customers in the smooth lime-inexperienced interior of Corte Farina. Choose among Argentinian empanadas (savory meat-stuffed pastries) and conventional pizzas, all of which are added to your table, piping warm from the oven. There's also outdoor seating in summertime.

Address: Central Verona, Via Corte Farina four, Verona, 37121

Telephone: +39 forty-five 800 0440.

Website: http://www.Cortefarina.It

Osteria Sottriva

Cuisine: Italian

Tucked underneath the entrances in a picturesque avenue, you may experience the warm temperature of

Sottoriva while you step inside the door. It dates back 300 years after they used to serve the sailors who labored the river Adige. Now, they plate up hearty dishes of meatballs, pasta with beans, and horsemeat stew to regulars and visitors alike. A handwritten observation acknowledges 'Servizio lento' (slow service), so sit again and loosen up.

Address: Sottoriva 10A, Verona, 37121

Telephone: +39 0.5 800 4124

Website: https://www.osteriaveronaantica.it/en/home

Verona Nightlife

Unlike Venice, its more conservative neighbour, Verona has a healthy but mature nightlife scene. Surrounded by wine-growing areas and a host of Italy's biggest annual wine honest, visitors will discover that bars and traditional stories (hotels) are enough. Many, moreover, host live music on the weekends.

Verona's club scene is modest. A handful of late-night spots dot the fringes of the metropolis, and plenty are small, compared to the mega-golf facilities of Rome and Naples. Their doors normally open at 2230 and fill up after nighttime.

Instead of clubs, Verona offers live suggestions by the bucketload. The summer opera and theatre festivals fill the city with visitors, and there may be a year-round programme of tunes, theatre, and dance at the metropolis's numerous theatres and ancient monuments.

Search the Spettacoli section of the nearby paper, L'Arena, or go to the traveller workplace for greater facts.

Bars in Verona

Caffè Filippini

The quality bar in town, Caffe Filippini, has served cocktails to a sophisticated crowd since 1901. Sit inside the traditional wood-panelled interior or at outside tables and try the house specialty, the Filippini cocktail, a combination of vermouth, gin, lemon, and ice. The bar is extremely lively on Friday and Saturday nights. For a more relaxed experience, consider stopping by for a leisurely pre-dinner café cornetto (coffee with grappa).

Address: Piazza Erbe 26, Verona, 37121

Telephone: +39 forty-five 800 4549.

Website: http://www.Caffefilippini.It

M27

Hip, younger locals make their way to this smart, funky bar for cold beers, music, and gossip. The selection of songs matches its slick, cool indoors, and the food is a contemporary take on Italian classics and some global dishes. The wine list is enormous and properly priced, and cocktails trade on an everyday basis.

Address: G Mazzini, 27, Verona, 37100

Telephone: +39 45 803 4242

Terrazza Bar Al Ponte

This fashionable wine bar regularly converts exhibitions from artists working domestically and similarly afield, along with impressive wine, chintzy cocktails, and hearty meals. Alongside the artistic endeavors are first-rate perspectives of the river and the Ponte Pietra with its fourteenth-century tower. The indoors has snug leather-primarily based-based totally seats and a snug environment; at the same time, the terrace is good for seeing the sun disappear.

Address: Ponte Piatra, 26, Verona, 37121

Telephone: +39 45 927 5032.

Website: http://www.Terrazzabaralponte.European

Victoria Club Bar

Part of the newly revamped Palazzo Victoria motel, this very clever bar offers some of Verona's cleverest cocktails to some of its greater in-the-recognize population. Service is seamless, the environment is snug, and clients are a thrilling blend of those staying upstairs and well-heeled locals. Victoria Club Bar is a wonderful location for an aperitivo earlier than dinner. It is best to retire if the nighttime time remains more youthful.

Address: Adua, eight, Verona, Verona 37121

Telephone: +39 half of 596 508

Website: http://www.Palazzovictoria.Com

Clubs in Verona

Alter Ego

Alter Ego is Verona's most well-known club, located in a quiet area in the Veronese hills. Small, it attracts a diverse crowd and DJs specializing in disco. The nice detail about it is the summer terrace, wherein you may dance the night away overlooking the backlit Verona.

Address: Torricelle 9, Verona, 37128

Telephone: +39 393 303 7766

Website: http://www.Alteregoclub.It/

Berfi's Club

One of Verona's older city-center membership venues, Berfi's, is small and intimate. It includes minimalist, white rooms: one supplying business, disco hits, and the opportunity, called the Caffe degli Artisti, in which there are ordinary stay performances. There is additionally an online eating place, and dinner is covered in the entrance fee.

Address: Lussemburgo 1, Verona, 37135

Telephone: +39 forty-five 508 024

Website: http://www.Berfis.Com

Hollywood Dance Club

This massive venue, positioned inside the path of Lake Garda, is younger Italy at its maximum glamorous and bubbling first-rate. Twenty-somethings from across the area flock proper here, particularly on Friday and Saturday nights, to bounce to the sounds of Italian superstars and massive international artists. Regularly converting DJs and first-rate cocktails are matched with unique dance nights and occasions.

Address: Bardolino, Via Montavoletta, eleven, Verona, 37011

Telephone: +39 45 511 8918

Website: http://www.Hollywood.It

Live music in Verona

Il Campidoglio

A lengthy-standing city favorite, Il Campiglio, off Piazza delle Erbe, is renowned for its tall cocktails and top-class Caribbean drinks. Happy hour, with generous aperitivi (snacks), is served from 1800-2100. The bar is split into halves: one catering to the live-tune crowd and some different, quieter consuming dens.

Address: Piazzetta Antonio Tirabosco 4, Verona, 37121

Telephone: +39 45 591 059.

Le Cantina del'Arena

For a few laid-lower returned live jazz – and a tremendous glass of wine – ebook a table at Cantina del'Arena. Styled as a track brasserie, the moody, brick interior and lengthy bar gadgets just the tone for leisurely strands of the saxophone. Order from the meat grill and quit with an entire-blooded glass of the neighbourhood Veneto Amarone.

Address: Piazetta Scalette Rubiani 1, Verona, 37121

Telephone: +39 45 803 2849

Website: http://www.Lecantine-area.Com

Classical track in Verona

Dance in Verona

Theatres in Verona

Teatro Filarmonico

The 18th-century Teatro Filarmonico is Verona's predominant venue for music and dramatic arts outside of the opera season. The Arena di Verona administers it and offers a complete complement of ballet, classical music, and opera. Occasionally, they also host live jazz and rock performances.

Address: dei Mutilati 4, Verona, 37121 Verona

Telephone: +39 45 800 5616

Website: http://www.Accademiafilarmonica.Org

Music and Dance in Verona

Culture in Verona

Verona Events

Bacanal del Gnoco (Verona Carnival)

Verona's carnival kicks off the year with many events and sports activities. It culminates on the day before Lent with a well-known parade in which many members wearing masked costumes walk through the streets together.

Date: 26 March 2023 - 26 March 2023

Venue: Throughout Verona

Cost:Free

Vinitaly

Vinitaly is Italy's most essential annual wine sincere. Hundreds of producers display the fantastic nearby wines amid wine-tasting lessons, enterprise conferences and seminars. Over 18s most effective.

Date: 02 April 2023 - 05 April 2023

Venue: Veronafiere

Website: https://www.Vinitaly.Com/

Italy Food and Drink

Italian delicacies, with their diverse local variations, outshine the well-known umbrella period on the Italian table. To the north, French and Austrian impacts make for dishes heavy in meat, cream, and butter, whilst further south, past the crucial area of Emilia-Romagna, the cooking turns lighter, centering round elements along with olive oil, tomatoes, and fish.

Locals are fiercely pleased with their regional specialties, each town or village proclaiming their local salami or cheese first-rate. Notable regional dishes include Neapolitan pizza, Milanese risotto, Sicilian sardines, Tuscan bean soup, Roman offal, Pugliese bread, Bolognese pasta, Parma ham and Piedmontese truffles.

The mystery of the path lies in the ingredients, which are selected with careful consideration for ripeness, texture, and flavor. So, devour the neighborhood and eat seasonal, and you will be tough pressed to have a bad meal.

Specialties

Gnocchi alla Romana: Known in English as Roman gnocchi, those dumplings are made from wealthy semolina dough.

Bagna càuda is a hot dipping sauce from Piedmont made with anchovies, garlic, olive oil, butter, and occasionally cream.

Pesto: A traditional Italian sauce combining basil, pine nuts and pecorino cheese.

Parmigiano-Reggiano: Also known as Parmesan cheese, this tough cow's milk cheese is regularly scraped onto plates.

Ossobuco: A Milanese bowl with veal shanks cooked in copious tomato and wine.

Ragù: A thick, slow-cooked meat sauce from Bologna served in lasagne with tagliatelle or other types of pasta.

Porchetta: A succulent red meat roast infused with herbs, garlic and fennel and encased in crackling pores and skin.

Panettone: An Italian Christmas cake with sultanas and candied fruit.

Limoncello: A lemon-flavored liqueur from Southern Italy, drank bloodless as a digestive.

Campari: A ruby-crimson-colored aperitif with a bittersweet flavor.

Wines: Celebrated Roman wines include frascati, pinot bianco and pinot grigio (whites); barolo, valpolicella, cabernet and pinot bero (reds). Wine regions of notice consist of Chianti, Montepulciano, and Brunello.

Tipping

Service costs and state taxes are covered in all restaurant payments. It is standard to give up to 10% in addition to if the provider has been right.

Drinking age

16 for beer and wine.

18 for distilled alcohol

CHAPTER 2
Travel To Verona

Flying To Verona

British Airways, easyJet and Ryanair provide direct flights to Verona from the United Kingdom. Cheap flights are available between December and Easter during the off-top season. If you are after a budget ruin, keep away from visiting during the summer season, especially July and August, as fees tend to soar in comparison with the rest of the 12 months. There are no direct flights from the United States.

Flight Schedules

From London - 2 hours

New York - 10 hours (including a stopover)

Los Angeles - thirteen hours 10 mins (including a stopover)

Toronto - 9 hours 40 mins (including a stopover)

Sydney - 25 hours (including stopovers).

Travel by using the road

The ancient center of Verona is a restrained traffic region (ZTL) from Monday to Friday from one thousand-

1330, 1600-1800 and 2000-2200, and from 1000-1330 on Saturday and Sunday.

Luckily, useful parks and rides fringe the city. The nearest vehicle park to the metropolis center is at Piazza Ciutadella. If you are staying in a city center, your inn can set up permission to drive into the restricted zone.

Traffic in Verona drives on the proper, and the minimal user age is eighteen. Speed limits are 130kph (80mph) on motorways, 90/110kph (56/68mph) on us of roads and 50kph (30mph) in urban areas. All those without an EU license must convey an International Driving Permit. A Green Card is useful, although now not compulsory for EU nationals.

The Automobile Club d'Italia (ACI) (Tel: +39 06 491 115; www.Aci.It) provides a beneficial advisory provider and can cope with breakdowns.

Emergency breakdown offerings

Automobile Club d'Italia (ACI) (Tel: +39 803 116).

Routes

Verona is positioned 160km (100 miles) east of Milan and 114km (75 miles) east of Venice. It is straightforward to attain either through taking the A4 toll road going for walks between Milan and Venice, exiting at Verona Sud, or using the A22 Brennero-Modena dual carriageway, once more exiting at Verona

Sud and following the signs and symptoms for the city center.

Coaches

ATV (Tel: +39 half 805 7811; www.Atv.Verona.It) operates buses from cities and villages within the Verona vicinity and from Lake Garda to the town center. It additionally organizes an airport commute from the railway station to Valerio Catullus Airport.

Coach services from other European cities are run via Euro lines (Tel: +39 0861 199 1900; www.Eurolines.It). They arrive and depart at Verona's Porta Nuova station.

Time to city

From Venice - 1 hour 25 minutes; Mantua - 40 minutes; Florence - 2 hours 40 minutes; Milan - 2 hours 10 minutes; Bologna - 1 hour 45 mins; Rome - 5 hours 15 min

Travel by Rail

Services

Rail offerings from Verona are innovative, dependable, and low-priced. The most important railway station in Verona is the Porta Nuova. It is positioned to the south of the town center. Both the Milan-Venice line and the Brennero-Rome line run through Porta Nuova.

Regular services also connect with Austria and Germany. You should buy tickets online for a paperless journey. You ought to validate the revealed tickets inside the yellow machines placed at the station structures prior to boarding.

Operators

Trenitalia (Tel: 89 20 21; www.Trenitalia.Com) is a countrywide rail corporation, which runs a quick, green, and excellent-value provider at some stage in Italy. It operates daily education services among Verona and all the main cities in northern Italy, as well as Florence and Rome.

Journey Times

From Venice - 1 hour 10 mins; Milan - 1 hour 25 mins; Florence - 2 hours 10 minutes; Rome - 3 hours 20 minutes; Munich - 5 hours 15 minutes; Vienna - 10 hours.

Transfer

There are frequent bus services from the railway station to the metropolis center.

Verona Hotels

Verona is a small town and is properly stocked with accommodation. When it involves precise patterns and budgets, there is an exquisite range of accommodations in Verona's historic center. During the opera season, rooms refill fast, so e-book nicely earlier.

The resorts under were hand-picked with the aid of our manual creator and are grouped into 3 pricing categories:

Luxury (over €200)

Moderate (€100 to €200)

Cheap (up to €100)

These are the starting costs for a double room and embody taxes and breakfast till otherwise designated.

Luxury

Escalus Luxury Suites

So, near the Arena, you could listen to the opera singers in the summertime if you fling the ground-to-ceiling windows open sufficiently. The modern-day Escalus Luxury Suites provide four-celebrity steeply priced with rooms designed by using Andrea Truglio. More rental than a motel, breakfast is added to your very own dining table every morning.

Address: Vicolo Tre Marchetti 12, Verona, 37121

Telephone: +39 45 803 6754.

Website: http://www.Escalusverona.Com

Gentlemen of Verona

Housed in a former 16th-century palace, the rooms here are more like residences. Each is styled, and they all ooze highly priced with parquet floors, Louis XVI chairs, modern-day bathrooms, and gold gilt frames among the excellent touches. Guests revel in herbal breakfasts in an inner courtyard garden. At the same time, a cigar room and an exceptional spa show lovable luxurious additions.

Address: Via Carlo Cattaneo, 26 A, Verona, 37121

Telephone: +39 45 800 9566.

Website: http://www.Thegentlemanofverona.Com

Do not forget this: Hotel Colomba d'Oro sits just a stone's throw away from the Adige River and the Arena, as well as being close to Romeo and Juliet's balcony. The hotel has fifty-one rooms. Each room is elegantly furnished with ornate mirrors, Italian artwork, and charming striped bedspreads. Visitors can enjoy a delicious breakfast buffet, and there is also a stylish cocktail bar on the premises.

Address: Via Cattaneo, 10, Verona, 37121

Telephone: +39 forty-five 595 three hundred.

Website: http://www.Colombahotel.Com

Moderate

Cinque Rooms

Located in a former butcher, this boutique bolt hole, near the Basilica di San Zeno Maggiore, has five drastically stylized rooms. There is not a reception region, so guests are sent a code for access as an alternative. With English floral fabrics, Swedish wallpaper, and godly king-period beds, this is a unique life for the rate.

Address: Piazzetta Portichetti 3, Verona, 37123

Telephone: +39 forty-five 597 004.

Website: http://www.Cinquerooms.It

Hotel Aurora

This establishment offers a welcoming atmosphere and a hospitable staff, making visitors feel right at home. Additionally, the charming terrace overlooking the main square, Piazza delle Erbe, provides a delightful view of Italy at its best. Not only does this 3-star hotel boast an exceptional location, but it also features 18 comfortable, air-conditioned rooms, each equipped with satellite TV.

Address: Piazzetta XIV Novembre, 2, Verona, 37121

Telephone: +39 45 594 717.

Website: http://www.Hotelaurora.Biz

Hotel Giulietta e Romeo

Enjoying a prominent position near the Arena and the number one buying streets, the 38 rooms of the Hotel Giulietta e Romeo are elegant and spotless. All encompass unfastened Wi-Fi and air-conditioning. The bounteous breakfast buffet can be worked off inside the small fitness room.

Address: Vicolo Tre Marchetti, three, Verona, 37121

Telephone: +39 45 800 3554.

Website: http://www.Giuliettaeromeo.It

Cheap

Hotel Torcolo

This friendly Inn in a vintage palazzo has an excessive region only some steps some distance from the Arena. Run with the aid of generous sisters; it is a face with the Opera crowd. The immoderate-ceilinged rooms are provided with wrought iron and antique beds, and all include air-conditioning and satellite television for PC TV.

Address: Vicolo Listone, three, Verona, 37121

Telephone: +39 45 800 7512.

Website: http://www.Hoteltorcolo.It

La Grotta Hotel

Remember this: La Grotta may not win any design awards with its jazzy bedspreads and fake Renaissance artwork on the walls, but it is a popular budget option with spacious rooms, a friendly staff, and complimentary minibar and Wi-Fi. Situated outside the city walls, it also offers free parking. It has a bus stop right outside the Inn for easy access to the city center.

Address: Strada Bresciana, sixteen, Verona, 37139

Telephone: +39 45 890 5702.

Website: http://www.Lagrottahotelvr.lt

Novo Hotel Rossi

Clean, priced and with loose bicycle hire, this resort is only a brief stroll from Verona's Verona's train station. While a few rooms are compact, all of them include satellite TV for PC TVs, air-conditioning, and Wi-Fi. The breakfast buffet is first-rate, too. Buses run regularly to the metropolis center in case you do not don't fancy the 20-minute walk.

Address: Via delle Coste 2, Verona, 37138

Telephone: +39 45 56 9022.

Website: http://www.Novohotelrossi.lt

CHAPTER 4
Italy Information

Travelling around Italy remains such an uncommon opinion in life – like an exquisite spring day or the electricity of past love – that may in no manner be publicized up. In a few locations, statistics, art, fashion, meals, and I. A. Dolce vita ("the best life") intermingle so outcomes.

In Italy, you will discover sunny isles, glacial lakes, and fiery volcanoes, rolling vineyards and concrete landscapes harboring more UNESCO World Heritage websites than a few different u. S. A. On Earth. Few places provide such variety, and few web page traffic go away without a genuine desire to go back.

The artistic and architectural wonders of Rome, Venice, Florence, and Naples attract visitors like magnets. Not satisfied with the Romans' conquest of most of the known world, the Venetians sent Marco Polo to unexplored lands. At the same time, Giotto, Leonardo da Vinci, Brunelleschi, and Michelangelo sparked the Renaissance in Western art and architecture.

Take in the beauty of the magnificent palaces, artwork, churches, and monuments. Marvel at the centuries of hard work and dedication to traditional techniques. Just like the local art, wine is also crafted to lift your spirits.

From the carefully constructed stone terraces of the Cinque Terre, snaking from sea level to breathtaking cliffs, to the sprawling hillsides of Chianti, the flatlands of the Po valley, and the volcanic slopes of Etna, Italian wines are lovingly made to complement the locally sourced cuisine on your plate.

Much like its food, this America is an infinite night meal of critiques. No matter how lots you gorge yourself, you will usually feel as though you are nonetheless on the primary route.

Do you cross-snowboarding within the Dolomites or biking in the United States of America? Do you dive into the solar-cut-up waters of Sardinia, climb Aeolian volcanoes or stalk market stalls in Naples? The preference is fantastic and bewildering. So, take the advice of the locals. Slow down, take a seat back, tuck in that serviette and get geared up to begin.

Italy Visa and Passport Requirements

Category			
EU	See below	No	No
USA	Yes	Yes	No
Canadian	Yes	Yes	No
Australian	Yes	Yes	No

| British | Yes | Yes | No |

Passports

E.U. nationals: You are not required to expose a passport or countrywide I.D. card whilst entering Italy. However, transport corporations like airways, train operators and ferry corporations could require you to reveal your passport or I.D. card to reveal your identification.

Non-EU nationals: To enter Italy, you must have a legitimate passport issued within the past ten years and with at least three months left, alongside a move-again ticket and sufficient finances during your stay.

Italy is a Schengen U. S., however, pays interest that E.U. individuals, which include Cyprus and Ireland, are not a part of the Schengen place, so a passport or I.D. card is required if touring to/from those countries.

Visas

E.U. nationals: You no longer want a visa for Italy if the life is much less than 90 days. Those who plan to stay longer will wish to have a residence.

Non-EU nationals: Nationals cited within the chart above (Americans, Australians, British and Canadians) can tour Italy and every other Schengen country without a visa for as much as ninety days in any given hundred and eighty-day length. However, this applies in terms of excursion as a visitor, to go to own family or friends, to attend employer conferences, cultural or sports. For other features, you need to test with the embassy, excessive commission or consulate of Italy in your own home U.S. What sort of visa and work permit do you want?

The complete listing of countries and territories whose nationals can visit Italy and some other Schengen international locations for as much as 90 days in any given hundred and eighty-day duration are below Antigua, Barbuda, Argentina, Australia, Bahamas, Barbados, Bosnia, Herzegovina, Brazil, Canada, Chile, Colombia, Costa Rica, Brunei, Dominica, Georgia, Grenada, Guatemala, Honduras, Hong Kong, Israel, Japan, Kiribati, Kosovo, Liechtenstein, Macao, Malaysia, El Salvador, Marshal Islands, Mauritius, Mexico, Micronesia, Montenegro, Nicaragua, Palau, Panama, Paraguay, Peru, North Macedonia, Saint Kitts and Nevis, Saint Lucia, Moldova, Saint Vincent, the Grenadines, Samoa, Seychelles, Singapore, Solomon Islands, Serbia, South Korea, Switzerland, Taiwan, Timor-Leste, Tonga, New Zealand, Trinidad. Tobago, Tuvalu, United Arab Emirates, United Kingdom, Ukraine, Uruguay, Vanuatu* and Venezuela, United States of America.

* Hong Kong and Macao: SAR passport holders no longer want a visa.

* Taiwan: holders of passports issued with the resources of Taiwan, which encompass an identification card range, do now not want a visa.

* Serbia: The Serbian Coordination Directorate-issued passport holders require visas, while the biometric passport holders do not anymore.

* Citizens of Vanuatu holding passports issued on or after 25 May 2015 are no longer required to obtain a visa.

• Nationals from micro-states interior the E.U. usa (Andorra, Monaco, San Marino, and Vatican City) additionally do no longer want a visa.

For nationals from nations now not listed right here, please contact the closest embassy to check the visa necessities for Italy.

Visa Note

For extra records about Schengen visas, have a look at the hyperlink to the item A manual to Schengen visas.

ETIAS travel authorization: Starting in mid-2025, all visitors who presently do now not need a visa to go to 30 European international locations will want to apply for an ETIAS adventure authorization.

Types and Cost

Schengen visa €eighty for folks who might be above 12 years old, €forty for children aged six to 12, and unfastened for children beneath six.

Nationals from Armenia, Azerbaijan and Kosovo pay €35.

In addition, the visa price is waived for the subsequent candidates:

• School pupils, college students, postgraduate college students and accompanying teachers who undertake remains for the motive of looking at instructional training.

• Researchers from 1/3 nations touring for the motive of carrying out medical studies.

• Representatives of non-income businesses elderly 25 years or tons less taking part in seminars, conferences, sports activities sports, cultural or educational activities organized with the aid of manner of non-earnings establishments.

• Family individuals of EU/EEA (European Economic Area) citizens, falling under Directive 2004/38.

Validity

Up to ninety days in any a hundred and eighty-day duration.

Transit

Citizens of some international locations want an airport transit visa while transiting via worldwide factors of any airports within the Schengen countries, whilst citizens of certain nations are exceptionally required a transit visa for a few of the Schengen international locations. If you are not from a Schengen visa-exempt U.S., please check with an Italian consulate near you.

Application to

Contact the embassy, immoderate commission, or consulate.

Schengen Visas

Italy is a Schengen usa, so the Schengen visa scheme applies.

Temporary residence

E.U. nationals: Will a house allow for added than ninety days?

Non-EU nationals: Will want a visa to stay in Italy for more than 90 days.

Working days

Schengen visa programs commonly take 15 to 21 calendar days: however, sometimes up to 45 days. Be privy to the national vacations in Italy, as they will affect the processing time. It is usually recommended to submit applications at least four weeks preceding to departure.

Sufficient Funds

Schengen visa candidates need to be able to provide evidence of a budget to cover their lives.

Extension of Stay

Schengen visa holders can only extend their visas for periods of less than ninety days under exceptional circumstances, such as in cases of force majeure or for humanitarian reasons.

Entry with pets

When bringing a puppy from every different E.U. usa of the United States, the animal should have a microchip or tattoo, an E.U. pet passport and a legitimate rabies vaccination certificate (the vaccination ought to have taken place at least 21 days before the journey). Animals from out of doors the E.U. must have an ISO 11784/11785 compliant 15-digit microchip additionally. Depending on whether your doggy is from an excessive-rabies United States of America or a rabies-controlled U. S.

Your puppy either desires to be vaccinated first or microchipped first. For pets from excessive-rabies global locations, a rabies titer looks at additionally must be administered 30 days after the vaccination. A veterinary certificate issued with the resource of a customary veterinarian is also required whilst coming into Italy with a puppy from outdoor of the E.U.

Please look at the consulate immediately for the perfect tactics.

This web page reflects our understanding of present-day rules for the most unusual forms of travel to the stated you. S. A. However, please phrase that every authority unit and forces entry guidelines; subsequently, we strongly advocate that you verify important statistics with the applicable embassy in advance of than excursion.

Embassies and traveller offices

Italian Embassy inside the USA

Telephone: +1 202 612 4400.

Website: http://www.Ambwashingtondc.Esteri.It

Address: 3000 NW Whitehaven Street, Washington DC, 20008,

Opening instances:

Mon-Fri 0900-1630 (visas through the usage of appointment simplest).

British Embassy in Italy

Telephone: +39 6 4220 0001.

Website: http://www.Gov.United nation/authorities/global/establishments/British-embassy-Rome

Address: Venti Settembre 80A, Rome, 00187,

Opening times:

By appointment satisfactory.

Italian Embassy within the U.K.

Telephone: +4420 7312 2200.

Website: http://www.Amblondra.Esteri.It

Address: Mayfair, 14 Three Kings Yard, London, W1K 4EH,

Opening instances:

By appointment, excellent.

Italy Health Care and Vaccinations

Yellow Fever	No
Typhoid	No
Tetanus	Yes
Rabies	No
Malaria	No
Hepatitis A	Yes
Diphtheria	Yes

Health Care

Travel insurance is suggested for all visitors. In a few medical instances, if you are European, you might be able to receive loose treatment if you can display evidence of a legitimate European Health Insurance Card (EHIC) obtained from your USA of foundation.

The normal standards of healthcare in Italy are wonderful. Hospitals and surgical procedures are nicely geared up, and personnel are talented. In pharmacies, over-the-counter recommendations are given, and widespread drug treatments are bought.

Food and Drink

Tap water is usually safe to drink, except in a few rural areas. If you see 'Acqua Non Potabile' written, it means the water is not drinkable. Most milk is pasteurized, and dairy products are safe to consume. Local meat, chicken, seafood, fruits, vegetables, and dairy items are all considered safe for consumption.

Other Risks

The World Health Organization (WHO) advises getting vaccinated against measles, mumps, rubella, polio, pertussis, pneumococcal disease, and hepatitis B.

Money and obligation unfastened for Italy.

Currency and Money

Currency information

Euro (EUR; image €) = 100 cents. Notes currencies are in denominations of €500, €200, €100, €50, €20, €10, and €5. Coins currencies are in denominations of 2 cents, 1 cent, 50 cents, 20, 10, 5, 2 and 1 cents.

Credit playing cards

Many places accept MasterCard, American Express, Cirrus, Maestro, and Visa. Some restaurants might add an extra "service fee" if you use a credit or debit card – it is best to ask them before paying with your card.

ATM

ATMs are extensively available at some point in Italy. Look for the 'Bancomat' sign for machines with multilingual interfaces. Pickpocketing and petty thievery can be elaborate in visitor areas, so take care to maintain property stability and be vigilant whilst making coin withdrawals.

Traveler's cheques

Traveler's cheques are not commonly accepted, even at banks, and typically incur high exchange fees. However, to avoid this, it is recommended that travelers obtain their cheques in Euros, Pounds Sterling, or US Dollars.

Banking hours

These vary from metropolis to metropolis but, in fashionable, Mon-Fri 0830-1330 and 1500-1600.

Currency regulations

There are no regulations on the import or export of neighborhood or foreign currency. However, quantities exceeding €10,000 or equal must be declared if visiting from or to a rustic outside the European Union.

Currency change

Foreign cash can be changed at banks, railway stations and airports and really frequently at fundamental motels (albeit typically at a much less advantageous exchange fee).

Italy duty lose

Italy is inside the European Union. Suppose you are touring from outdoor of the EU. In that case, you are entitled to shop for perfume, skincare, cosmetics, Champagne, wine, decided on spirits, style accessories, gifts, and souvenirs - all at tax-unfastened equivalent fees.

Italy's responsibility-loose allowance for travelers from EU countries:

If you are over 17 years old, you're free to buy and take items with you when travelling among EU nations, furnished that you have paid tax on those goods and they're in your very own use (now not for sale). However, if you deliver in more than the subsequent, customs officials are likely to impeach you:

- 800 cigarettes or 400 cigarillos or 2 hundred cigars or 1kg of tobacco.

- 90L of nonetheless wine (60L of sparkling wine).

- 110L of beer.

• 10L of alcoholic liquids more potent than 22% or 20L of fortified or glowing wine or other liqueurs up to 22%.

Beware that each EU United States has distinctive regulations for visitors under 17 years old. Please check before your journey.

Italy's obligation-loose allowance for travelers from non-EU countries:

Suppose you are arriving from a non-EU United States of America. In that case, the subsequent goods can be imported into Italy with the aid of visitors with a minimal age of 17 years without incurring customs duty:

• 200 cigarettes or a hundred cigarillos (max. 3 grams every) or 50 cigars or 250g of tobacco. You may additionally combine any of those tobacco merchandise provided you no longer exceed the entire restriction.

• 4L of wine, 16L of beer and 1L of spirits over 22% volume or 2L of alcoholic drinks less than 22% quantity or a proportional mix of those products furnished, the restrict is not exceeded.

• Other items as much as the value of €430 for air and sea visitors and €300 for other travelers (decreased to €150 for youngsters below 15).

Banned Imports

Meat, fish and milk and any derivative products from most non-EU countries blanketed animal and plant species, unlicensed firearms and guns, and counterfeit items.

Banned Exports

An export license must follow cultural artefacts that are greater than 50 years antique.

CONCLUSION

As our journey through Verona ends, we hope you have experienced the city's unique blend of history, culture, and modern vibrancy. From the iconic Arena di Verona, where the echoes of ancient performances still resonate, to the romantic allure of Juliet's Balcony, the city invites you to explore its rich tapestry of stories and legends.

Strolling through the narrow, cobblestone streets, you have likely felt the centuries of history shaping this enchanting city. Verona's architectural marvels, such as the majestic Castelvecchio and its numerous churches' serene beauty, testify to its storied past. Each monument, each piazza, tells a tale of a bygone era, inviting you to immerse yourself in the splendor of a city that has been a crossroads of cultures and traditions.

The culinary delights of Verona, from the hearty dishes of Valpolicella to the delicate pastries of the local Pasticceria, have surely left a lasting impression on your palate. The city's food and wine are not just sustenance but an integral part of its cultural identity, offering a sensory journey through the flavors of the Veneto region.

As you reflect on your time in Verona, we hope you carry with you the memories of its vibrant festivals, the warmth of its people, and the breathtaking views from its ancient bridges. Verona is more than a destination; it is an experience, a place where the past and present coexist harmoniously, creating an atmosphere that is both timeless and inviting.

We encourage you to take the spirit of Verona, a city that celebrates love, art, and history with an unparalleled passion. Whether it's the tranquil moments by the Adige River or the bustling energy of Piazza delle Erbe, let Verona's charm inspire you long after you leave its storied streets.

Thank you for allowing us to guide you through this remarkable city. Until your next visit, arrivederci, and may your travels continue to be filled with discovery and wonder.

Printed in Great Britain
by Amazon

46020893R00056